Fantastic Bundt cake recipes for every generation!

Indulgent flavors for your occasions

Table of Contents

Introduction

Making Bundt cakes can be fun and enjoyable in every household. You can make Bundt cakes for any special occasion, for a memorable holiday like Christmas or New Year's Eve, or even on a warm summer night to enjoy with your favorite people.

These mouthwatering desserts can be served with a chocolate glaze or sliced with a dollop of whipped cream mixed with honey or maple syrup. The ingredients are fundamental, and you probably have a lot of them in your kitchen pantry, so grab a bowl, whip up the Bundt cake batter and enjoy this fantastic dessert perfect for any occasion.

Some recipes have the most incredible presentation, so don't be surprised if your guests ask for the recipe—one exciting thing about it. Bundt cake batter can be used as a muffin butter and make perfect muffins or cupcakes. Yum!

1. Classic Bundt Cake Recipe

This classic recipe is adorable and easy to follow. You will love the soft and delicious taste of this amazing.

Time: 60 minutes

Servings: 12

The list of ingredients:

- 1 1/2 cups softened butter
- 1 1/2 cups granulated sugar

- 6 large eggs, room temperature

- 2 1/2 teaspoons baking powder

- pinch of salt

- 3 cups all-purpose flour

- 1 tablespoon vanilla extract

- 3/4 cup whole milk

Methods:

Step 1

In a large mixing bowl, beat the butter with the granulated sugar.

Step 2

Stir in the eggs and mix until thoroughly combined. Scarpe down the sides of the bowl if needed.

Step 3

Stir in the vanilla extract and milk and mix until combined.

Step 4

Finally, add the flour, baking powder, and salt and mix until well combined.

Step 5

Grease a Bundt cake pan with butter or vegetable oil and add the batter to the prepared pan.

Step 6

Bake in an already heated oven at 350 F or 180 C degrees for about 40-45 minutes.

Step 7

Cover the Bundt cake with a piece of aluminum foil if needed after 30 minutes.

Step 8

Cool down completely before serving.

2. Chocolate Bundt Cake Recipe

If you love chocolate desserts, you will love this Bundt cake recipe. It's fantastic and perfect for breakfast or dessert on a fancy special occasion.

Time: 60 minutes

Servings: 12

The list of ingredients:

- 1 1/2 cups softened butter

- 1 1/2 cups granulated sugar

- 6 large eggs, room temperature

- 2 1/2 teaspoons baking powder

- pinch of salt

- 3 cups all-purpose flour

- 1 tablespoon vanilla extract

- 3/4 cup almond milk

- 8 oz melted dark chocolate

Methods:

Step 1

In a large mixing bowl, beat the butter with the granulated sugar.

Step 2

Stir in the eggs and mix until thoroughly combined. Scarpe down the sides of the bowl if needed.

Step 3

Stir in the vanilla extract and almond milk and mix until combined.

Step 4

Finally, add the flour, baking powder, and salt, and mix until well combined. Finally, stir in the melted dark chocolate.

Step 5

Grease a Bundt cake pan with butter or vegetable oil and add the batter to the prepared pan.

Step 6

Bake in an already heated oven at 350 F or 180 C degrees for about 40-45 minutes.

Step 7

Cover the Bundt cake with a piece of aluminum foil if needed after 30 minutes.

Step 8

Cool down completely before serving.

3. Chocolate Hazelnut Bundt Cake Recipe

The chocolate hazelnut flavor is one of the most adored in the world. You will love this Bundt cake recipe as one of the best you have ever tried.

Time: 60 minutes

Servings: 12

The list of ingredients:

- 1 1/2 cups softened butter
- 1 1/2 cups granulated sugar
- 6 large eggs, room temperature
- 2 1/2 teaspoons baking powder
- pinch of salt
- 2 1/2 cups all-purpose flour
- 1/2 cup cocoa powder
- 1 tablespoon vanilla extract
- 3/4 cup whole milk
- 1 cup chopped hazelnuts

Methods:

Step 1

In a large bowl, beat the butter with the brown sugar.

Step 2

Stir in the eggs and mix until thoroughly combined. Scarpe down the sides of the bowl if needed.

Step 3

Stir in the vanilla extract and whole milk and mix until combined.

Step 4

Finally, add the flour, cocoa powder, baking powder, and salt and mix until well combined. Finally, stir in the chopped hazelnuts.

Step 5

Grease a Bundt cake pan with butter or vegetable oil and add the batter to the prepared pan.

Step 6

Bake in an heated oven at 350 F or 180 C degrees for about 40-45 minutes.

Step 7

Cover the Bundt cake with a piece of aluminum foil if needed after 30 minutes.

Step 8

Cool down completely before serving.

4. Chocolate and caramel Bundt cake recipe

Chocolate and caramel are one of the best flavors, and this Bundt cake is proof of that. It's easy to follow, and you will enjoy it with the whole family.

Time: 60 minutes

Servings: 12

The list of ingredients:

- 1 1/2 cups softened butter
- 1 1/2 cups granulated sugar
- 6 large eggs, room temperature
- 2 1/2 teaspoons baking powder
- pinch of salt
- 3 cups all-purpose flour
- 1 tablespoon vanilla extract
- 3/4 cup whole milk
- 8 oz. melted dark chocolate
- 5 tablespoons caramel sauce

Methods:

Step 1

In a large mixing bowl, beat the butter with the granulated sugar.

Step 2

Stir in the eggs and mix until thoroughly combined. Scarpe down the sides of the bowl if needed.

Step 3

Stir in the vanilla extract and whole milk and mix until combined.

Step 4

Finally, add the flour, baking powder, and salt and mix until well combined. Finally, stir in the melted dark chocolate.

Step 5

Grease a Bundt cake pan with butter or vegetable oil and add the batter to the prepared pan.

Step 6

Drizzle the caramel sauce, and using a toothpick, make swirls to insert the caramel sauce into the Bundt cake batter.

Step 7

Bake in an heated oven at 350 F or 180 C degrees for about 40-45 minutes.

Step 8

Cover the Bundt cake with a piece of aluminum foil if needed after 30 minutes.

Step 9

Cool down completely before serving.

5. Chocolate and Nutella Bundt cake

This recipe is fantastic and rich in chocolate flavor. You will adore every bite; the kids will enjoy this Bundt cake the most.

Time: 60 minutes

Servings: 12

The list of ingredients:

- 1 1/2 cups softened butter

- 1 1/2 cups granulated sugar

- 6 large eggs, room temperature

- 2 1/2 teaspoons baking powder

- pinch of salt

- 3 cups all-purpose flour

- 1 tablespoon vanilla extract

- 3/4 cup whole milk

- 1 cup Nutella

Methods:

Step 1

In a large mixing bowl, beat the butter with the granulated sugar.

Step 2

Stir in the eggs and mix until thoroughly combined. Scarpe down the sides of the bowl if needed.

Step 3

Stir in the vanilla extract and whole milk and mix until combined.

Step 4

Finally, add the flour, baking powder, and salt and mix until well combined. Finally, stir in the Nutella.

Step 5

Grease a Bundt cake pan with butter or vegetable
oil and add the batter to the prepared pan.

Step 6

Bake in a heated oven at 350 F or 180 C degrees for
about 40-45 minutes.

Step 7

Cover the Bundt cake with a piece of aluminum foil
if needed after 30 minutes.

Step 8

Cool down completely before serving.

6. Chocolate and almond Bundt cake

This recipe is fantastic and rich in chocolate flavor. You will adore every bite; the kids will enjoy this Bundt cake the most.

Time: 60 minutes

Servings: 12

The list of ingredients:

- 1 1/2 cups softened butter

- 1 1/2 cups granulated sugar

- 6 large eggs, room temperature

- 2 1/2 teaspoons baking powder

- pinch of salt

- 3 cups all-purpose flour

- 1 tablespoon vanilla extract

- 3/4 cup whole milk

- 7 oz. melted chocolate

- 3/4 cup chopped almonds

Methods:

Step 1

In a large mixing bowl, beat the margarine with the granulated sugar.

Step 2

Stir in the eggs and mix until thoroughly combined. Scarpe down the sides of the bowl if needed.

Step 3

Stir in the vanilla extract and whole milk and mix until combined.

Step 4

Finally, add the flour, baking powder, and salt and mix until well combined. Finally, stir in the melted chocolate and chopped almonds.

Step 5

Grease a Bundt cake pan with butter or vegetable oil and add the batter to the prepared pan.

Step 6

Bake in a heated oven at 350 F or 180 C degrees for about 40-45 minutes.

Step 7

Cover the Bundt cake with a piece of aluminum foil if needed after 30 minutes.

Step 8

Cool down completely before serving.

7. Chocolate and peanut butter Bundt cake

This amazing flavor combination is just gorgeous. You will love the rich chocolate flavor combined together with the smooth peanut butter.

Time: 60 minutes

Servings: 12

The list of ingredients:

- 1 1/2 cups softened butter
- 1 1/2 cups granulated sugar
- 6 large eggs, room temperature
- 2 1/2 teaspoons baking powder
- pinch of salt
- 3 cups all-purpose flour
- 1 tablespoon vanilla extract
- 3/4 cup whole milk
- 7 oz. melted chocolate
- 3 tablespoons peanut butter

Methods:

Step 1

In a large mixing bowl, beat the margarine with the granulated sugar.

Step 2

Stir in the eggs and mix until thoroughly combined. Scarpe down the sides of the bowl if needed.

Step 3

Stir in the vanilla extract and whole milk and mix until combined.

Step 4

Finally, add the flour, baking powder, and salt and mix until well combined. Finally, stir in the melted chocolate and peanut butter.

Step 5

Grease a Bundt cake pan with butter or vegetable oil and add the batter to the prepared pan.

Step 6

Bake in a heated oven at 350 F or 180 C degrees for about 40-45 minutes.

Step 7

Cover the Bundt cake with a piece of aluminum foil if needed after 30 minutes.

Step 8

Cool down completely before serving.

8. Chocolate and almond butter Bundt cake

Another nut butter-inspired delicious Bundt cake is this almond butter and yummy chocolate flavor combination.

Time: 60 minutes

Servings: 12

The list of ingredients:

- 1 1/2 cups softened butter

- 1 1/2 cups granulated sugar

- 6 large eggs, room temperature

- 2 1/2 teaspoons baking powder

- pinch of salt

- 3 cups all-purpose flour

- 1 tablespoon vanilla extract

- 3/4 cup almond milk

- 7 oz melted chocolate

- 3 tablespoons almond butter

Methods:

Step 1

In a large mixing bowl, beat the margarine with the granulated sugar.

Step 2

Stir in the eggs and mix until thoroughly combined. Scarpe down the sides of the bowl if needed.

Step 3

Stir in the vanilla extract and almond milk and mix until combined.

Step 4

Finally, add the flour, baking powder, and salt and mix until well combined. Finally, stir in the melted chocolate and almond butter.

Step 5

Grease a Bundt cake pan with butter or vegetable oil and add the batter to the prepared pan.

Step 6

Bake in a heated oven at 350 F or 180 C degrees for about 40-45 minutes.

Step 7

Cover the Bundt cake with a piece of aluminum foil if needed after 30 minutes.

Step 8

Cool down completely before serving.

9. Chocolate and marzipan Bundt cake

Marzipan bundt cake is always a delicious and fantastic flavor combination, perfect for any occasion. You will enjoy this Bundt cake with hot tea, warm milk, and a cup of coffee.

Time: 60 minutes

Servings: 12

The list of ingredients:

- 1 1/2 cups softened butter
- 1 1/2 cups granulated sugar
- 6 large eggs, room temperature
- 2 1/2 teaspoons baking powder
- pinch of salt
- 3 cups all-purpose flour
- 1 tablespoon vanilla extract
- 3/4 cup almond milk
- 7 oz melted chocolate
- 3 oz. marzipan softened

Methods:

Step 1

In a large mixing bowl, beat the margarine and marzipan with the granulated sugar.

Step 2

Stir in the eggs and mix until thoroughly combined. Scarpe down the sides of the bowl if needed.

Step 3

Stir in the vanilla extract and almond milk and mix until combined.

Step 4

Finally, add the flour, baking powder, and salt and mix until well combined. Finally, stir in the melted chocolate and mixture.

Step 5

Grease a Bundt cake pan with butter or vegetable oil and add the batter to the prepared pan.

Step 6

Bake in a heated oven at 350 F or 180 C degrees for about 40-45 minutes.

Step 7

Cover the Bundt cake with a piece of aluminum foil if needed after 30 minutes.

Step 8

Cool down completely before serving.

10. Chocolate and sour cherries Bundt cake

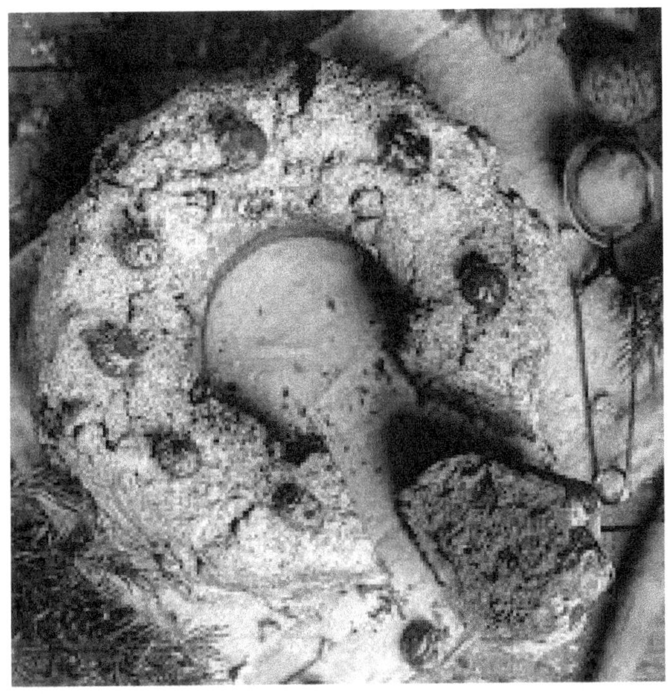

Chocolate and sour cherries are one of the most excellent flavor combinations ever. You will love this rich and indulgent flavor.

Time: 60 minutes

Servings: 12

The list of ingredients:

- 1 1/2 cups softened butter
- 1 1/2 cups granulated sugar
- 6 large eggs, room temperature
- 2 1/2 teaspoons baking powder
- pinch of salt
- 3 cups all-purpose flour
- 1 tablespoon vanilla extract
- 3/4 cup sour cream
- 7 oz melted chocolate
- 1 cup sour cherries

Methods:

Step 1

In a large mixing bowl, beat the butter with the granulated sugar.

Step 2

Stir in the eggs and mix until thoroughly combined. Scarpe down the sides of the bowl if needed.

Step 3

Stir in the vanilla extract and sour cream and mix until combined.

Step 4

Finally, add the flour, baking powder, and salt and mix until well combined. Finally, stir in the melted chocolate and sour cherries.

Step 5

Grease a Bundt cake pan with butter or vegetable oil and add the batter to the prepared pan.

Step 6

Bake in a heated oven at 350 F or 180 C degrees for about 40-45 minutes.

Step 7

Cover the Bundt cake with a piece of aluminum foil if needed after 30 minutes.

Step 8

Cool down completely before serving.

11. Honey Bundt Cake Recipe

If you like floral essence to your Bundt cake, you will adore this fantastic recipe. It's perfect for any occasion.

Time: 60 minutes

Servings: 12

The list of ingredients:

- 1 1/2 cups softened butter
- 1 1/2 cups granulated sugar

- 6 large eggs, room temperature
- 2 1/2 teaspoons baking powder
- pinch of salt
- 3 cups all-purpose flour
- 1 tablespoon vanilla extract
- 3/4 cup whole milk
- 3 tablespoons honey

Methods:

Step 1

In a large mixing bowl, beat the butter with the granulated sugar.

Step 2

Stir in the eggs and mix until thoroughly combined. Scarpe down the sides of the bowl if needed.

Step 3

Stir in the vanilla extract and milk and mix until combined.

Step 4

Finally, add the flour, baking powder, and salt and mix until well combined.

Step 5

Stir in the honey and mix until combined.

Step 6

Grease a Bundt cake pan with butter or vegetable oil and add the batter to the prepared pan.

Step 7

Bake in an already heated oven at 350 F or 180 C degrees for about 40-45 minutes.

Step 8

Cover the Bundt cake with a piece of aluminum foil if needed after 30 minutes.

Step 9

Cool down completely before serving.

12. Honey and walnut Bundt Cake Recipe

Honey and walnuts are one of the best flavors you will find out there. You will enjoy this combination because it's perfect for summertime.

Time: 60 minutes

Servings: 12

The list of ingredients:

- 1 1/2 cups softened butter

- 1 1/2 cups granulated sugar

- 6 large eggs, room temperature

- 2 1/2 teaspoons baking powder

- pinch of salt

- 3 cups all-purpose flour

- 1 tablespoon vanilla extract

- 3/4 cup whole milk

- 3 tablespoons honey

- 1 cup chopped walnuts

Methods:

Step 1

In a large mixing bowl, beat the butter with the granulated sugar.

Step 2

Stir in the eggs and mix until thoroughly combined. Scarpe down the sides of the bowl if needed.

Step 3

Stir in the vanilla extract and milk and mix until combined.

Step 4

Finally, add the flour, baking powder, and salt and mix until well combined.

Step 5

Stir in the honey and chopped walnuts and mix until combined.

Step 6

Grease a Bundt cake pan with butter or vegetable oil and add the batter to the prepared pan.

Step 7

Bake for 40 to 45 minutes at 350 °F or 180 °C in a preheated oven.

Step 8

Cover the Bundt cake with a piece of aluminum foil if needed after 30 minutes.

Step 9

Cool down completely before serving.

13. Maple syrup Bundt Cake Recipe

You will adore this maple syrup-inspired Bundt cake recipe, which is one of the best flavors you will enjoy. You will enjoy this the most with a cup of milk or coffee.

Time: 60 minutes

Servings: 12

The list of ingredients:

- 1 1/2 cups softened butter

- 1 1/2 cups granulated sugar

- 6 large eggs, room temperature

- 2 1/2 teaspoons baking powder

- pinch of salt

- 3 cups all-purpose flour

- 1 tablespoon vanilla extract

- 3/4 cup whole milk

- 3 tablespoons maple syrup

Methods:

Step 1

In a large mixing bowl, beat the butter with the granulated sugar.

Step 2

Stir in the eggs and mix until thoroughly combined. Scarpe down the sides of the bowl if needed.

Step 3

Stir in the vanilla extract and milk and mix until combined.

Step 4

Finally, add the flour, baking powder, and salt and mix until well combined.

Step 5

Stir in the maple syrup.

Step 6

Grease a Bundt cake pan with butter or vegetable oil and add the batter to the prepared pan.

Step 7

Bake in a heated oven at 350 F or 180 C degrees for about 40-45 minutes.

Step 8

Cover the Bundt cake with a piece of aluminum foil if needed after 30 minutes.

Step 9

Cool down completely before serving.

14. Maple syrup and pecans Bundt Cake Recipe

Do you know what goes well with maple syrup? Pecans are the answer. You will enjoy this flavor combination the most and enjoy every bite of this Bundt cake dessert.

Time: 60 minutes

Servings: 12

The list of ingredients:

- 1 1/2 cups softened butter
- 1 1/2 cups granulated sugar
- 6 large eggs, room temperature
- 2 1/2 teaspoons baking powder
- pinch of salt
- 3 cups all-purpose flour
- 1 tablespoon vanilla extract
- 3/4 cup whole milk
- 3 tablespoons maple syrup
- 3/4 cup chopped pecans

Methods:

Step 1

In a large mixing bowl, beat the butter with the granulated sugar.

Step 2

Stir in the eggs and mix until thoroughly combined. Scarpe down the sides of the bowl if needed.

Step 3

Stir in the vanilla extract and milk and mix until combined.

Step 4

Finally, add the flour, baking powder, and salt and mix until well combined.

Step 5

Stir in the maple syrup and chopped pecans.

Step 6

Grease a Bundt cake pan with butter or vegetable oil and add the batter to the prepared pan.

Step 7

Bake in a heated oven at 350 F or 180 C degrees for about 40-45 minutes.

Step 8

Cover the Bundt cake with a piece of aluminum foil if needed after 30 minutes.

Step 9

Cool down completely before serving.

15. Coconut Bundt Cake Recipe

Enjoy the flavor of the coconut in this Bundt cake recipe and share it with your favorite people. You are going to love this fantastic recipe.

Time: 60 minutes

Servings: 12

The list of ingredients:

- 1 1/2 cups softened butter

- 1 1/2 cups granulated sugar

- 6 large eggs, room temperature

- 2 1/2 teaspoons baking powder

- pinch of salt

- 3 cups all-purpose flour

- 1 tablespoon vanilla extract

- 3/4 cup coconut milk

- 1/4 cup coconut flakes

Methods:

Step 1

In a large mixing bowl, beat the butter with the granulated sugar.

Step 2

Stir in the eggs and mix until thoroughly combined. Scarpe down the sides of the bowl if needed.

Step 3

Stir in the vanilla extract and coconut milk and mix until combined.

Step 4

Finally, add the flour, baking powder, and salt and mix until well combined.

Step 5

Stir in the coconut flakes.

Step 6

Grease a Bundt cake pan with butter or vegetable oil and add the batter to the prepared pan.

Step 7

Bake in a heated oven at 350 F or 180 C degrees for about 40-45 minutes.

Step 8

Cover the Bundt cake with a piece of aluminum foil if needed after 30 minutes.

Step 9

Cool down completely before serving.

16. Rum Bundt Cake Recipe

If you want your Bundt cake to be delicious and for adults only, then a touch of rum will infuse its flavor base and be perfect for entertaining.

Time: 60 minutes

Servings: 12

The list of ingredients:

- 1 1/2 cups softened butter

- 1 1/2 cups granulated sugar

- 6 large eggs, room temperature

- 2 1/2 teaspoons baking powder

- pinch of salt

- 3 cups all-purpose flour

- 1 tablespoon vanilla extract

- 3/4 cup whole milk

- 1/4 cup dark rum

Methods:

Step 1

In a large mixing bowl, beat the butter with the granulated sugar.

Step 2

Stir in the eggs and mix until thoroughly combined. Scarpe down the sides of the bowl if needed.

Step 3

Stir in the vanilla extract and whole milk and mix until combined.

Step 4

Finally, add the flour, baking powder, and salt and mix until well combined.

Step 5

Stir in the dark rum and mix until combined.

Step 6

Grease a Bundt cake pan with butter or vegetable oil and add the batter to the prepared pan.

Step 7

Bake in a heated oven at 350 F or 180 C degrees for about 40-45 minutes.

Step 8

Cover the Bundt cake with a piece of aluminum foil if needed after 30 minutes.

Step 9

Cool down completely before serving.

17. Crushed Oreo Bundt Cake Recipe

Oreo cookies are perfect for every dessert, but this Bundt cake pan is a delicious way to enjoy them even more.

Time: 60 minutes

Servings: 12

The list of ingredients:

- 1 1/2 cups softened butter
- 1 1/2 cups granulated sugar

- 6 large eggs, room temperature
- 2 1/2 teaspoons baking powder
- pinch of salt
- 3 cups all-purpose flour
- 1 tablespoon vanilla extract
- 3/4 cup whole milk
- 20 crushed Oreo cookies

Methods:

Step 1

In a large mixing bowl, beat the butter with the granulated sugar.

Step 2

Stir in the eggs and mix until thoroughly combined. Scarpe down the sides of the bowl if needed.

Step 3

Stir in the vanilla extract and whole milk and mix until combined.

Step 4

Finally, add the flour, baking powder, and salt and mix until well combined.

Step 5

Stir in the crushed Oreo cookies and mix until combined.

Step 6

Grease a Bundt cake pan with butter or vegetable
oil and add the batter to the prepared pan.

Step 7

Bake in a heated oven at 350 F or 180 C degrees for
about 40-45 minutes.

Step 8

Cover the Bundt cake with a piece of aluminum foil
if needed after 30 minutes.

Step 9

Cool down completely before serving.

18. Graham cracker Bundt Cake Recipe

If you like a white version of crushed cookies in your Bundt cake, you will adore this following flavor combination – vanilla and graham crackers.

Time: 60 minutes

Servings: 12

The list of ingredients:

- 1 1/2 cups softened butter
- 1 1/2 cups granulated sugar
- 6 large eggs, room temperature
- 2 1/2 teaspoons baking powder
- pinch of salt
- 3 cups all-purpose flour
- 1 tablespoon vanilla extract
- 3/4 cup whole milk
- 1 1/2 cups crushed graham crackers

Methods:

Step 1

In a large mixing bowl, beat the butter with the granulated sugar.

Step 2

Stir in the eggs and mix until thoroughly combined. Scarpe down the sides of the bowl if needed.

Step 3

Stir in the vanilla extract and whole milk and mix until combined.

Step 4

Finally, add the flour, baking powder, and salt and mix until well combined.

Step 5

Stir in the crushed graham crackers and mix until combined.

Step 6

Grease a Bundt cake pan with butter or vegetable oil and add the batter to the prepared pan.

Step 7

Bake in a heated oven at 350 F or 180 C degrees for about 40-45 minutes.

Step 8

Cover the Bundt cake with a piece of aluminum foil if needed after 30 minutes.

Step 9

Cool down completely before serving.

19. Chocolate chips Bundt Cake Recipe

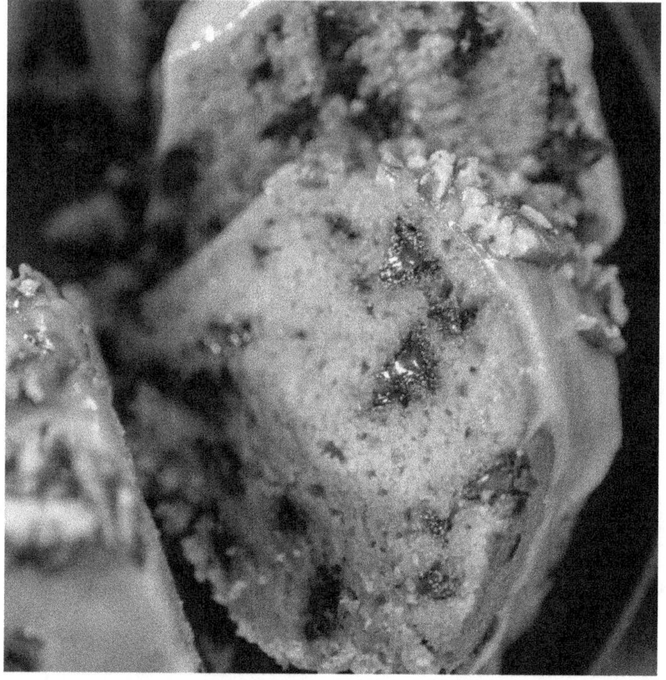

This vanilla-inspired Bundt cake has that chocolate chips in the batter, and you will love every bite of this adorable dessert.

Time: 60 minutes

Servings: 12

The list of ingredients:

- 1 1/2 cups softened butter
- 1 1/2 cups granulated sugar
- 6 large eggs, room temperature
- 2 1/2 teaspoons baking powder
- pinch of salt
- 3 cups all-purpose flour
- 1 tablespoon vanilla extract
- 3/4 cup whole milk
- 1 1/2 cups chocolate chips

Methods:

Step 1

In a large mixing bowl, beat the butter with the granulated sugar.

Step 2

Stir in the eggs and mix until thoroughly combined. Scarpe down the sides of the bowl if needed.

Step 3

Stir in the vanilla extract and whole milk and mix until combined.

Step 4

Finally, add the flour, baking powder, and salt and mix until well combined.

Step 5

Stir in the chocolate chips and fold until combined.

Step 6

Grease a Bundt cake pan with butter or vegetable oil and add the batter to the prepared pan.

Step 7

Bake in a heated oven at 350 F or 180 C degrees for about 40-45 minutes.

Step 8

Cover the Bundt cake with a piece of aluminum foil if needed after 30 minutes.

Step 9

Cool down completely before serving.

20. White chocolate chips and chocolate Bundt Cake Recipe

This Bundt cake recipe is dark chocolate and you will enjoy white chocolate chips into the batter well combined. Yum!

Time: 60 minutes

Servings: 12

The list of ingredients:

- 1 1/2 cups softened butter

- 1 1/2 cups granulated sugar

- 6 large eggs, room temperature

- 2 1/2 teaspoons baking powder

- pinch of salt

- 2 1/2 cups all-purpose flour

- 1/2 cup cocoa powder

- 1 tablespoon vanilla extract

- 3/4 cup whole milk

- 1 1/2 cups white chocolate chips

Methods:

Step 1

In a large mixing bowl, beat the butter with the granulated sugar.

Step 2

Stir in the eggs and mix until thoroughly combined. Scarpe down the sides of the bowl if needed.

Step 3

Stir in the vanilla extract and whole milk and mix until combined.

Step 4

Finally, add the flour, baking powder, cocoa powder and salt and mix until well combined.

Step 5

Stir in the white chocolate chips and fold until
combined.

Step 6

Grease a Bundt cake pan with butter or vegetable
oil and add the batter to the prepared pan.

Step 7

Bake in a heated oven at 350 F or 180 C degrees for
about 40-45 minutes.

Step 8

Cover the Bundt cake with a piece of aluminum foil
if needed after 30 minutes.

Step 9

Cool down completely before serving.

21. Strawberry Bundt Cake Recipe

This yummy Bundt cake is fantastic and delicious, especially when you bite into the delightful and rich diced strawberries. You can always serve this Bundt cake with powdered sugar.

Time: 60 minutes

Servings: 12

The list of ingredients:

- 1 1/2 cups softened butter
- 1 1/2 cups granulated sugar
- 6 large eggs, room temperature
- 2 1/2 teaspoons baking powder
- pinch of salt
- 3 cups all-purpose flour
- 1 tablespoon vanilla extract
- 3/4 cup sour cream
- 1 1/2 cups diced strawberries

Methods:

Step 1

In a large mixing bowl, beat the butter with the granulated sugar.

Step 2

Stir in the eggs and mix until thoroughly combined. Scarpe down the sides of the bowl if needed.

Step 3

Stir in the vanilla extract and sour cream and mix until combined.

Step 4

Finally, add the flour, baking powder, and salt and mix until well combined.

Step 5

Stir in the diced strawberries and fold until combined.

Step 6

Grease a Bundt cake pan with butter or vegetable oil and add the batter to the prepared pan.

Step 7

Bake in a heated oven at 350 F or 180 C degrees for about 40-45 minutes.

Step 8

Cover the Bundt cake with a piece of aluminum foil if needed after 30 minutes.

Step 9

Cool down completely before serving.

22. Blueberry Bundt Cake Recipe

You will enjoy this fantastic recipe for Bundt cake with juicy blueberries. The flavor is always excellent if you add them fresh, but you can always use frozen.

Time: 60 minutes

Servings: 12

The list of ingredients:

- 1 1/2 cups softened butter

- 1 1/2 cups granulated sugar

- 6 large eggs, room temperature

- 2 1/2 teaspoons baking powder

- pinch of salt

- 3 cups all-purpose flour

- 1 tablespoon vanilla extract

- 3/4 cup Greek yogurt

- 1 1/2 cups fresh blueberries

Methods:

Step 1

In a large mixing bowl, beat the butter with the granulated sugar.

Step 2

Stir in the eggs and mix until thoroughly combined. Scarpe down the sides of the bowl if needed.

Step 3

Stir in the vanilla extract and Greek yogurt and mix until combined.

Step 4

Finally, add the flour, baking powder, and salt and mix until well combined.

Step 5

Stir in the fresh blueberries and fold until combined.

Step 6

Grease a Bundt cake pan with butter or vegetable oil and add the batter to the prepared pan.

Step 7

Bake in a heated oven at 350 F or 180 C degrees for about 40-45 minutes.

Step 8

Cover the Bundt cake with a piece of aluminum foil if needed after 30 minutes.

Step 9

Cool down completely before serving.

23. Blueberry and lemon Bundt Cake Recipe

Did you know that blueberries and lemon are one of the best flavor combinations? You can add lemon juice and zest to the classic vanilla batter and transform the whole recipe into a decadent and delicious dessert.

Time: 60 minutes

Servings: 12

The list of ingredients:

- 1 1/2 cups softened butter

- 1 1/2 cups granulated sugar

- 6 large eggs, room temperature

- 2 1/2 teaspoons baking powder

- pinch of salt

- 3 cups all-purpose flour

- 1 tablespoon vanilla extract

- 3/4 cup Greek yogurt

- 1 1/2 cups fresh blueberries

- zest and juice of 1 lemon

Methods:

Step 1

In a large mixing bowl, beat the butter with the granulated sugar.

Step 2

Stir in the eggs and mix until thoroughly combined. Scarpe down the sides of the bowl if needed.

Step 3

Stir in the vanilla extract and Greek yogurt and mix until combined.

Step 4

Finally, add the flour, baking powder, and salt and mix until well combined.

Step 5

Stir in the fresh blueberries, lemon juice, and zest and fold until combined.

Step 6

Grease a Bundt cake pan with butter or vegetable oil and add the batter to the prepared pan.

Step 7

Bake in a heated oven at 350 F or 180 C degrees for about 40-45 minutes.

Step 8

Cover the Bundt cake with a piece of aluminum foil if needed after 30 minutes.

Step 9   Cool down completely before serving.

24. Raspberry Bundt Cake Recipe

This is another fruit-inspired Bundt cake recipe that is so easy to put together. The fresh raspberries will give a delicious and rich taste to the classic vanilla Bundt cake batter.

Time: 60 minutes

Servings: 12

The list of ingredients:

- 1 1/2 cups softened butter
- 1 1/2 cups granulated sugar
- 6 large eggs, room temperature
- 2 1/2 teaspoons baking powder
- pinch of salt
- 3 cups all-purpose flour
- 1 tablespoon vanilla extract
- 3/4 cup Greek yogurt
- 1 1/2 cups fresh or frozen raspberries

Methods:

Step 1

In a large mixing bowl, beat the butter with the granulated sugar.

Step 2

Stir in the eggs and mix until thoroughly combined. Scarpe down the sides of the bowl if needed.

Step 3

Stir in the vanilla extract and Greek yogurt and mix until combined.

Step 4

Finally, add the flour, baking powder, and salt and mix until well combined.

Step 5

Stir in the fresh or frozen raspberries.

Step 6

Grease a Bundt cake pan with butter or vegetable oil and add the batter to the prepared pan.

Step 7

Bake in a heated oven at 350 F or 180 C degrees for about 40-45 minutes.

Step 8

Cover the Bundt cake with a piece of aluminum foil if needed after 30 minutes.

Step 9

Cool down completely before serving.

25. Banana bread Bundt Cake Recipe

If you love good banana bread, you will love this fantastic Bundt cake recipe with mashed bananas.

Time: 60 minutes

Servings: 12

The list of ingredients:

- 1 1/2 cups softened butter
- 1 1/2 cups granulated sugar

- 6 large eggs, room temperature

- 2 1/2 teaspoons baking powder

- pinch of salt

- 3 cups all-purpose flour

- 1 tablespoon vanilla extract

- 3/4 cup Greek yogurt

- 3 mashed bananas

Methods:

Step 1

In a large mixing bowl, beat the butter with the granulated sugar.

Step 2

Stir in the eggs and mix until thoroughly combined. Scarpe down the sides of the bowl if needed.

Step 3

Stir in the vanilla extract and Greek yogurt and mix until combined.

Step 4

Finally, add the flour, baking powder, and salt and mix until well combined.

Step 5

Stir in the mashed bananas into the batter and mix until combined.

Step 6

Grease a Bundt cake pan with butter or vegetable oil and add the batter to the prepared pan.

Step 7

Bake in a heated oven at 350 F or 180 C degrees for about 40-45 minutes.

Step 8

Cover the Bundt cake with a piece of aluminum foil if needed after 30 minutes.

Step 9

Cool down completely before serving.

26. Pineapple Bundt Cake Recipe

The following recipe is full of flavor and rich in taste because it has crushed pineapple pieces in the batter, and you will love every bite of it.

Time: 60 minutes

Servings: 12

The list of ingredients:

- 1 1/2 cups softened butter

- 1 1/2 cups granulated sugar

- 6 large eggs, room temperature

- 2 1/2 teaspoons baking powder

- pinch of salt

- 3 cups all-purpose flour

- 1 tablespoon vanilla extract

- 3/4 cup whole milk

- 1 14 oz can drained crush pineapple

Methods:

Step 1

In a large mixing bowl, beat the butter with the granulated sugar.

Step 2

Stir in the eggs and mix until thoroughly combined. Scarpe down the sides of the bowl if needed.

Step 3

Stir in the vanilla extract and whole milk and mix until combined.

Step 4

Finally, add the flour, baking powder, and salt and mix until well combined.

Step 5

Stir in the crushed pineapple into the batter and mix until combined.

Step 6

Grease a Bundt cake pan with butter or vegetable oil and add the batter to the prepared pan.

Step 7

Bake in a heated oven at 350 F or 180 C degrees for about 40-45 minutes.

Step 8

Cover the Bundt cake with a piece of aluminum foil if needed after 30 minutes.

Step 9

Cool down completely before serving.

27. Pineapple and Coconut Bundt Cake Recipe

The classic pina colada flavor can be delicious and perfectly made in a Bundt cake version, and this one is so delicious. Perfect for every occasion, even if you are a beginner in cooking, you will make it without extra effort.

Time: 60 minutes

Servings: 12

The list of ingredients:

- 1 1/2 cups softened butter
- 1 1/2 cups granulated sugar
- 6 large eggs, room temperature
- 2 1/2 teaspoons baking powder
- pinch of salt
- 3 cups all-purpose flour
- 1 tablespoon vanilla extract
- 3/4 cup coconut milk
- 1 14 oz can drained crush pineapple
- 1/2 cup coconut flakes

Methods:

Step 1

In a large mixing bowl, beat the butter with the granulated sugar.

Step 2

Stir in the eggs and mix until thoroughly combined. Scarpe down the sides of the bowl if needed.

Step 3

Stir in the vanilla extract and coconut milk and mix until combined.

Step 4

Finally, add the flour, baking powder, and salt and mix until well combined.

Step 5

Mix the crushed pineapple and coconut flakes into the batter until combined.

Step 6

Grease a Bundt cake pan with butter or vegetable oil and add the batter to the prepared pan.

Step 7

Bake in a heated oven at 350 F or 180 C degrees for about 40-45 minutes.

Step 8

Cover the Bundt cake with a piece of aluminum foil if needed after 30 minutes.

Step 9

Cool down completely before serving.

28. Cinnamon Bundt Cake Recipe

One of the best classic fall flavors is this delicious cinnamon Bundt cake recipe that can be made almost all fall and winter in your kitchen. It's rich in flavor and full of delicious taste.

Time: 60 minutes

Servings: 12

The list of ingredients:

- 1 tablespoon vanilla extract

- 1 1/2 cups softened butter

- 3 cups all-purpose flour

- 3/4 cup whole milk

- 2 1/2 teaspoons baking powder

- 2 tablespoons ground cinnamon

- 1 1/2 cups granulated sugar

- pinch of salt

- 6 large eggs, room temperature

Methods:

Step 1

In a large mixing bowl, beat the butter with the granulated sugar.

Step 2

Stir in the eggs and mix until thoroughly combined. Scarpe down the sides of the bowl if needed.

Step 3

Stir in the vanilla extract and whole milk and mix until combined.

Step 4

Finally, add the flour, baking powder, and salt and mix until well combined.

Step 5

Mix the ground cinnamon into the batter until combined.

Step 6

Grease a Bundt cake pan with butter or vegetable oil and add the batter to the prepared pan.

Step 7

Bake in a heated oven at 350 F or 180 C degrees for about 40-45 minutes.

Step 8

Cover the Bundt cake with a piece of aluminum foil if needed after 30 minutes.

Step 9

Cool down completely before serving.

29. Cinnamon and apple Bundt Cake Recipe

Apples are delicious fruit during the fall and winter, and you can dice them into small cubes or grate them finely and stir them into the Bundt cake batter to have the best apple Bundt cake recipe ever.

Time: 60 minutes

Servings: 12

The list of ingredients:

- 1 1/2 cups softened butter
- 1 1/2 cups granulated sugar
- 6 large eggs, room temperature
- 2 1/2 teaspoons baking powder
- pinch of salt
- 3 cups all-purpose flour
- 1 tablespoon vanilla extract
- 3/4 cup whole milk
- 1 tablespoon ground cinnamon
- 2 peeled and grated apples

Methods:

Step 1

In a large mixing bowl, beat the butter with the granulated sugar.

Step 2

Stir in the eggs and mix until thoroughly combined. Scarpe down the sides of the bowl if needed.

Step 3

Stir in the vanilla extract and whole milk and mix until combined.

Step 4

Finally, add the flour, baking powder, and salt and mix until well combined.

Step 5

Mix the ground cinnamon and grated apple into the batter until combined.

Step 6

Grease a Bundt cake pan with butter or vegetable oil and add the batter to the prepared pan.

Step 7

Bake in a heated oven at 350 F or 180 C degrees for about 40-45 minutes.

Step 8

Cover the Bundt cake with a piece of aluminum foil if needed after 30 minutes.

Step 9

Cool down completely before serving.

30. Pear Bundt Cake Recipe

Another great flavor combination is this pear and vanilla Bundt cake recipe. Perfect for entertaining and during the wintertime.

Time: 60 minutes

Servings: 12

The list of ingredients:

- 1 1/2 cups softened butter

- 1 1/2 cups granulated sugar

- 6 large eggs, room temperature

- 2 1/2 teaspoons baking powder

- pinch of salt

- 3 cups all-purpose flour

- 1 tablespoon vanilla extract

- 3/4 cup whole milk

- 2 grated pears

Methods:

Step 1

In a large mixing bowl, beat the butter with the granulated sugar.

Step 2

Stir in the eggs and mix until thoroughly combined. Scarpe down the sides of the bowl if needed.

Step 3

Stir in the vanilla extract and whole milk and mix until combined.

Step 4

Finally, add the flour, baking powder, and salt and mix until well combined.

Step 5

Mix the grated pears into the batter until combined.

Step 6

Grease a Bundt cake pan with butter or vegetable oil and add the batter to the prepared pan.

Step 7

Bake in a heated oven at 350 F or 180 C degrees for about 40-45 minutes.

Step 8

Cover the Bundt cake with a piece of aluminum foil if needed after 30 minutes. Cool down completely before serving.

Conclusion

Whether your favorite flavor is vanilla or chocolate or even some fruit-inspired Bundt cakes, you will enjoy every

bite of these amazing desserts served over the holidays or al fresco dinner on a warm summer night.

You can add some chopped nuts to the Bundt cake batter and enjoy the crunchiness in every bite. You will adore these flavors.

I hope this book will find its way to your kitchen and help you master the art of making Bundt cakes.

www.ingramcontent.com/pod-product-compliance
Lightning Source LLC
Chambersburg PA
CBHW071545150726
48000CB00002B/943